Whitebait and Wetlands

Whitebait and Wetlands

Tales of the West Coast

John Dawson and David Henshaw

David Bateman

First published in 1998 by
David Bateman Ltd, 30 Tarndale Grove,
Albany, Auckland, New Zealand

ISBN 1 86953 3941

Designed by Chris O'Brien/Pages Literary Pursuits
Printed by Ideal Print LTD,
Auckland

Contents

Acknowledgements

The authors acknowledge the following sources and people who have assisted:
Ron and Marion Ferguson; *Stories of the Fox-Paringa-Haast Road*, published by
the Re Union Committee 1995, Chairman Maurice Roberts; *The Wild West Coast*
by Leslie Hobbs ['Coaster Pat' reproduced with the permission of Penguin Books
(NZ) Ltd]; Four Winds Charlie Glass and Joan; Brian and Veronica Chinn; John
Gerald Birchfield; Charlie Stewart and Sid Wilson; Graham 'Frosty' Steel; Fraser
Hughson; Bernie Dowrick; the late Roy Anderson; Thomas Condon; Don and
Diane Bradley; Bill Tacon; Pat Fitzgerald; Jack O'Donnell; Norma Liner; Tony
Connors; Ian Robb; Hec Sinclair; Steve Nelson; Vince Peterson and Dave 'Shaggy
Dogs' Marshall; Rex Hudson, Arthur Barakat and the Morrinsville RSA.

For encouragement and feedback: Tim Johnston, Gary Craig, Bill Ritchie.

Preface

This is an illustrated collection of tales that the authors have heard on the West Coast. Some of the stories are completely factual and were witnessed, participated in or recounted first-hand to the authors. Others are partly factual and have been appropriately embellished for the telling. A few cannot be verified at all, but are part of the folklore of the West Coast and so are included on that basis. All, it can be safely said, were heard on the West Coast.

Obviously, names have been changed, and sometimes localities. The few genuine names of living West Coasters are all used with their permission. It should be understood that if a name used is that of a living person, then it is pure coincidence and no offence is intended.

We hope you enjoy the book.

Introduction

The West Coast is a unique part of New Zealand. Unique in its geography — a long coastal strip between the Southern Alps and the Tasman Sea, crossed by rivers and shrouded in rain forest; unique in its history of gold and coal mining, land development and forestry. But most importantly, unique in its people, their attitudes, their characteristics and their humour.

In the 1970s the two authors were appointed to the Coast, fresh out of Massey and Lincoln Universities, and keen to leave their mark on the place. Both were involved in the farming industry, travelled widely and grew to know and respect the Coast — and the Coasters.

The jury is still out on whether they made their mark on the Coast, but one thing is sure, the Coast made a permanent mark on them.

This book is dedicated to the Coast and the Coasters. We hope it depicts something of this special place, its people and the events which simply wouldn't happen anywhere else. For the Coaster is blessed with a sense of humour and perspective, unique in itself.

We hope you agree . . .

John Dawson and David Henshaw

1 The Opening of the Wanganui River Bridge

In an area where rivers dominate life, the opening of a new bridge is a major event. So it was with the opening of the Wanganui River bridge at Hari Hari in 1963. South Westland was there in force, with most of the locals between Ross and Fox Glacier present for the big day. It was also one of local officialdom's memorable occasions, with the local M.P., the Westland County Council, the Mayor of Hokitika, and local representatives of the Hospital Board all in attendance. To complete the picture, there was an assortment of local businessmen, contractors, sawmillers and stock agents. Most were accompanied by their wives — all adorned in their 'Sunday best'.

Appropriately, the opening ceremony was a great success and the official party, following afternoon tea and celebratory drinks, embarked upon the trip back to Hokitika, stopping, as is the custom, at every pub on the way. Their trip would take them through stops at Lake Ianthe, Ross (two pubs), Woodstock and Kaniere.

The entourage was led by the Hokitika mayoral limousine with the Mayor and his splendidly attired wife, who sat regally in the back seat, with her good friend the wife of the local M.P. Consistent with her reputation as the best dressed woman on the Coast, her entire outfit had been purchased from Harrods, with the exception of the high-heeled crocodile-skin shoes which came from Dior in Paris. She was quite a landmark in Hokitika and a

talking-point at all female gatherings. It would be true to say that the airs and graces of the Mayoress were not consistent with Coasters' expectations of the Mayor's wife. This inconsistency ensured that she was frequently the butt of local humour. A fact she remained blissfully unaware of.

It took fifteen minutes to get to the Pukekura Tavern at Lake Ianthe. The 'Puke Tavern' is an old sawmill pub set forty metres off the main road amongst the magnificent rimu forest which the highway bisects. It is easily missed by passing traffic and, continually shaded by the forest, when in winter the road can be icy and dangerous. The pub sits in front of a swamp and a derelict sawmill — the sort visitors like to photograph or sketch. Its appearance epitomises what it is — a once-bustling outfit now unmaintained, dirty and slowly fading into oblivion. Rather like the mill behind it.

Still, it was a red letter day for the 'Puke Pub'. At four o'clock its ample fire was roaring, and the long bar was packed with Coast dignitaries. For the ex-mill worker owner, Christmas had come early, delivering a far more salubrious clientele than the possum trappers, farmers and contractors who comprised his regulars.

Three such locals sat quietly in the corner. Ned Sadler, Herb Chinn and Michael Nolan watched the proceedings with amusement. They were all from the Waitaha Valley, just five minutes north of the pub. Ned Sadler was a possum trapper and whitebaiter, Herb Chinn farmed Herefords while Michael Nolan owned the local bulldozer doing Catchment Board, logging and land-clearing work. They were all from well-known Coast families.

It was Herb Chinn who overheard the Mayoress of Hokitika ask where the 'Ladies' was. "I'll show you," the landlord replied, leading her out of the bar and along the verandah before pointing to a solitary outhouse some 50 metres from the back of the pub behind the swamp. The Mayoress blanched at the prospect. It was primitive, it was public and it looked smelly! The only access was over the swamp via the 'slab path'. This was a series of slab timber lengths which made a pathway between the verandah steps and the ladies' longdrop.

As the Mayoress picked her way across the slab path in her crocodile-skin high heels, Ned Sadler, Herb Chinn and Michael Nolan could not control their mirth, and they moved outside for a better look. It was Ned Sadler who spotted the half-brick in the rushes. In an instant he grabbed it and said, "Let's give her a fright". As he heaved the brick, the others watched expectantly.

In the ladies' longdrop facilities were just not up to standard. The lack of paper and presence of large spiders caused a change of mind. The Mayoress would cross her legs until Ross. As she opened the door to head back, the brick, travelling in a graceful arc, spiralled towards her.

It hit her fair between the eyes, and knocked her backwards into the longdrop.

The trio looked at each other aghast, rooted to the spot in fear. They wanted to run, but their legs wouldn't move. "You've bloody well killed her!" yelled Herb. Ned surveyed the scene in horror, his eyes coming to rest on the crocodile-skin high heels, now motionless, which was all he could see of the Lady Mayoress. The rest of her lay in the darkness of the longdrop. Then he did what any red-blooded Coaster would do under the circumstances — he ran!!

It is 225 kilometres from the Puke Pub to Haast. Ned Sadler gave himself up twenty-three days later. He had travelled through thick bush, climbed bluffs and swum rivers. He was exhausted, bloody and contrite.

* * *

Surprisingly, the Mayoress was not seriously injured, and recovered consciousness on the way to Ross. Eight careful stitches and time restored her striking good looks. Shortly afterwards her husband was defeated at the local body elections. They retired over the hill at Rangiora and she no longer attends bridge openings.

The police at Haast did not charge Ned Sadler as they could not find a suitable charge. He no longer heaves bricks at ladies' longdrops.

The Puke Pub is still serving beer and the new owner painted it in 1972. A busload of Japanese tourists stopped there in 1983. A ladies' loo was added in 1984. Ned Sadler, Herb Chinn and Michael Nolan still drink at the Pukekura Tavern.

Michael and Herb still enjoy recounting the events of the day the Wanganui bridge was opened.

2 The Poacher

Mick Fitzpatrick lived near Atarau on the northern side of the Grey River. Here he ran the family sheep and beef farm with his brother Leo. Both were bachelors and hard workers, but kept pretty much to themselves. Leo was more extroverted than Mick, and had gained some notoriety by poaching deer and trout and supplying one of the hotels in Greymouth with 'game'.

Unfortunately, Mick had none of his brother's guile, and was quite clumsy and leaden-footed when accompanying his shadowy brother in the early days. He had long since been left behind, and he resented it. So he decided to do something about it. While he was always going to be a crook shot, he reckoned that he had seen enough of geligniting trout to become proficient and that this might give him some status around the place. Besides, he was envious of his brother's 'off farm' income.

One day after much thought and planning, Mick raided the gelignite supply and headed for the large hole by the spur groyne in the Grey River at the back of the property. Carefully, he rehearsed the sequence: 'Light the fuse, count to three, drop it into the river.' After a couple of dress rehearsals, he was ready to go.

Nervously he lit the fuse, counted to three, and threw the matchbox into the river!

Some people still marvel that Mick survived the blast. With his arm badly damaged, his face lacerated and his ears ringing, Mick staggered back to the house and was quickly rushed to Grey Hospital. The blast had done enormous damage, but he did survive. He lost an arm, the sight in his left eye and required extensive skin grafts to the side of his face. He was also stone deaf in his left ear.

It was only hours after the accident that the local ranger got to hear of Mick's misfortune. At the earliest opportunity he visited Mick in hospital, who ruefully admitted the poaching attempt. Three days later, to everyone's horror, Mick Fitzpatrick was charged with poaching trout in the Grey River at Atarau.

There have been few acts in the Grey Valley which have caused such a community backlash and expression of revulsion as the charging of Mick Fitzpatrick on this occasion. Certainly, poaching was a problem. But to choose to make a test case out of an instance where a man was nearly killed, despite the publicity it would generate and the messages it would send, was simply beyond the pale.

At the court case six months later, Mick Fitzpatrick was represented by local lawyer Mr Dick Maidenhead. In front of circuit judge Geoffrey Morrison, Maidenhead put forward a guilty plea but asked the court for a discharge due to the 'extenuating circumstances'. The courtroom anticipated a lengthy account of the personal injuries incurred by Mick Fitzpatrick, ending up with the conclusion that he had been punished enough through injury for his offence.

But no such submission was made. Instead Dick Maidenhead Q.C. submitted: "Your Honour, my plea for discharge is based on provocation. We do not deny that the accused was poaching trout using explosives — simply that he was provoked to the point where any reasonable man would have acted similarly."

"In what way was he provoked?" asked Judge Morrison curiously.

Maidenhead replied, "The accused has a vegetable garden near the river concerned, and at night the trout were slithering through the grass and eating his lettuces."

The court was silent, although wry looks and raised eyebrows were widespread. Finally the Judge replied.

"Well that sounds like provocation enough for me. Case dismissed."

Mick Fitzpatrick returned to full fitness and active farming. He impressed everyone with his unfailing good humour, and would recount the poaching incident in the pub with full acting and gestures. He died in his fifties, still a bachelor and is fondly remembered. Much more fondly than the ranger who took him to court and was transferred to the North Island a few months later.

3 Vicar's Folly

Marty Pask was for some years the best dairy farmer in Hari Hari. What was more admirable was his apprenticeship, which involved a range of forestry and contracting jobs. He was then a bus driver for the Railways doing the South Westland run. While he was bus driving, Marty started rearing a few calves on a vacant section in Hari Hari. Encouraged and assisted by his wife Jane this grew to the purchase of a small block, and then to a small dairy farm in 1961. Both of them had a natural ability with livestock and were tidy and methodical. They were also keen to learn and worked hard. Together they were a formidable team, with their mown tanker track, gardens around the cowshed and always freshly painted buildings reflecting their pride in the farm.

Since 1961 they steadily expanded their operation, buying adjacent land and continually increasing production. Throughout it all Marty emerged as the most admired dairy farmer in the district. In addition to his farming achievements his quick wit and colourful turn of phrase livened all gatherings.

In the '70s, Marty was an enthusiastic organiser and participant in annual Discussion Group tours, which took place immediately after the cows dried off in mid May. It was in this role that I got to know him well as room mate and co-organiser of these trips.

One night Marty confided to me that he would be prepared to trade all his wealth for the ability to read and write. I was amazed to hear that he was illiterate, and asked him how he managed to cope and disguise it. "Well, Jane does the bookwork, writes the cheques and letters. I either book things up or pay cash. We manage quite well really.... Except on the odd occasion — like last Sunday."

And then unfolded the story of the vicar's folly.

In the early '70s Hari Hari got a new vicar. He was a well bred Englishman, and recently married to an exquisite French girl, upon whom, apparently, he did not dote enough. After a miserable few months, the vicar's French wife met and fell in love with the one and only Willy Tunnicliffe. If ever there was a 'likeable rogue' in South Westland it was Willy, sire of eleven kids and owner of an undeveloped block upon which he grew rushes and ran a decent sized mob of Hereford cows whose calves he sold at the annual calf sale at Whataroa. He was also a very good pilot and owned his own plane.

It was as a result of a scenic flight with the vicar's French wife that the relationship began. After a few weeks it had developed into a raging passionate affair which culminated when they disappeared in Willy's plane.

Hari Hari was aghast — especially coming hard on the heels on the high school wife-swapping scandal. The Canterbury Diocese felt the same and promptly transferred the hapless vicar back to Christchurch.

And so a new vicar was appointed to Hari Hari. Jane Pask, who was also the Parish Secretary, welcomed the